T0207894

HOLY BLOOD TRANSFUSION

WENDELL GILKEY

WESTBOW
PRESS®
A DIVISION OF THOMAS NELSON
& ZONDERVAN

WestBow Press books may be ordered through booksellers or by contacting:

WestBow Press
A Division of Thomas Nelson & Zondervan
1663 Liberty Drive
Bloomington, IN 47403
www.westbowpress.com
844-714-3454

Scripture taken from the King James Version of the Bible.

ISBN: 978-1-6642-3192-4 (sc)
ISBN: 978-1-6642-3191-7 (e)

Library of Congress Control Number: 2021908331

Print information available on the last page.

WestBow Press rev. date: 05/28/2021

CONTENTS

AUTHOR'S NOTE

Kudos to you! Congratulations on purchasing this unique workbook. You are about to embark on one of the most important adventures of your life. This is the beginning of an extremely critical and necessary undertaking. It is critical to you and to your descendants as well.

This is not a chore that you have to muddle through; it is a very satisfying and enlightening experience. When I did this for myself, I became very excited about being able to wake up and continue each day—and you will too!

This is your own personal workbook. It is not just a read; it is a very valuable tool that you will use to move this process forward in your life. This book is not to be shared with others. It will contain very private information about you. Go ahead and mark it up, make notes in it, and highlight things for future reference. This book was not intended to be used with a practitioner, a facilitator, or a mentor. It is intended for you to go one on one with the Lord himself privately. It does not matter if you're a baby Christian or a mature Christian; it is written for everyone. And it does not matter which denomination or church you go to; if you love Jesus, this book is for you.

This book will facilitate your journey in these areas:

> confessing of your sins
> repenting for your sins
> asking forgiveness for your sins, as you forgive yourself
> confessing for your ancestors' sins
> repenting for their sins
> asking forgiveness for their sins
> forgiving those who have trespassed against you
> forgiving your ancestors for the harm they have caused you and your family

This workbook is to stay with you for your entire life. Use it to make touch-ups as you go through life. Do not let personal sins, ancestral sins, and forgiveness pile up on you.

I personally use the pay-as-you-go plan. I confess, repent, and forgive regularly. I do not wait for my prayer time; I do this on my feet.

Even after you are finished, additional ancestral sins will probably be brought to mind. Just deal with them in the moment.

Nothing takes the place of reading the Bible for yourself. Never depend on anyone else to tell you what is in the Bible. You are supposed to read it for yourself. Ask the Holy Spirit to help you understand it, and he will. You don't need the commentaries. You have the Holy Spirit to guide you, but you have to *ask* him! You will understand it as you go; I guarantee it.

You do not need a read-the-Bible-in-one-year plan. I know people who read the Bible seven times a year. I have read it in just a few months. I started out in the New Testament and read it through like a book all the way to Revelation. Well, that was interesting and enjoyable, and I learned so much. The Bible is alive; it is the Living Word of God. If it is the Word of God, and you believe that it is, it is only reasonable that you will read it all the way through and study it, right?

After reading the New Testament, I went to Psalms and Proverbs and read them through, going slowly enough that I understood each one of them. I took the time to let it all soak in. I asked for the Holy Spirit to lead me into all truth every day.

By the time I got to Genesis, reading the entire Bible was no longer a formidable task. It was now absolutely doable. I really enjoyed Genesis, and I took my time and found it to be more interesting than a best-selling novel. I went from Genesis all the way through to the end of the Old Testament, and I was really enjoying the read. I woke up one day to find that I had completely read the Bible for myself at my pace, and I had understood what I had read.

I wish I had the wisdom and knowledge in this workbook when I was young because I would have been miles ahead of anyone else. I would have avoided many pitfalls and problems. I have written this book at this time to give you the heads-up and enlighten you about the truth.

So, enjoy this book—and may you be at peace and be anxious about nothing. May the Lord bless and keep you. May he make his face shine upon you and give you grace and peace. Amen.

INTRODUCTION

I know you love your children, your grandchildren, and your great-grandchildren. If you're like me, you want to leave them in good shape during your lifetime and after your passing. You would not purposefully pass on any negative thing to them. You would not leave them in crushing debt or leave a huge mess for them to inherit and have to clean up.

However, every time you sin against God, you are doing just that: leaving a generational curse upon them down to the third and fourth generation. If you only realized that you're not just hurting yourself but your descendants as well, you might not take sin so lightly. You are hurting the very people you love the most *as* you sin in your lifetime. You are harming them in real time.

I know you pray for your loved ones, and many of you pray for them unceasingly each and every day. I know your descendants have problems that you ask God to intervene in, but in many cases, their problems do not seem to go away. You ask yourself, "Why are my prayers not being answered—or how am I praying wrong?"

The answer may lie in the fact that generational curses are real. They have affected your life, both your parents' lives, their parents' lives, and your progeny's lives. However, the buck can stop with you.

In this book, I show you the solution as it was given to me by the Holy Spirit. I show you step-by-step how to "clear and clean" your blood and put a stop to generational curses and inherited diseases. I will lead you into personal repentance, the forgiveness of others, and forgiving your ancestors for the damage they have caused to you and your family.

You will learn to fear the Lord and have a healthy respect for him and his statutes. How do you qualify? By observing his commandments and listening to his voice. You will avoid sin at all costs because it is paid for with an incredibly high price by you — and by your descendants.

My prayer is that you will use this God-given knowledge to break the generational curses in your lives, repent for your own personal sins, and forgive all who have trespassed against you. It is not enough to just pray, "I break all the generational curses in my life." Believe me, I have done that for years, and it just does not cut it. This, my dear saints, will cut it. It did it for me, and it will for you.

A Vision

As I was praying at my residence in the early morning, I asked, "What do you want to show me today, Lord?" When I looked up, I saw a vision on the wall just above my television. It was of my two ancestral lines going all the way back to Adam. My father's line was on my left, and my mother's line was on my right. There was a great divide between them that came together. I heard a voice in my spirit, and it said, "This is the point of your insertion."

As I was looking at my ancestors, I kept noticing two dark lumps in front of me. I kept trying to figure out what they were, and then I realized they were my knees, which was what I would see if I were sitting and looking down. At that point, I saw that I was indeed seated and looking forward at this amazing vision of my ancestral lines. I recognized my mother on the right side, and I saw my grandparents behind her. I did not recognize the other people behind them. The same held true for my father's side. I recognized my father and his parents but not the others.

The divide between the two groups became wider the further back in time that it represented. The divide was the land. There were two canyons in the land, and that was where I saw my ancestors. They were shown to me as thousands of people stretching back for thousands of miles and thousands of years as far as I could see. On both sides, they were separated by a section of land that was elevated so that they could not see the other group. I realized that this huge pool of the two peoples contained my DNA and my blood. It also contained my iniquities, my twists and bends, and my talents and abilities. My physical body and everything about me were determined by these two peoples, including my temperament, desirable traits, and undesirable traits.

I saw two founts coming toward me, one from each group, and they looked like three-quarter-inch tubes. The tubes came together at my presence. I knew that any inherited diseases were contained in these founts—as well as any judgments of almighty God, upon my ancestors, which would affect me down to the third and fourth generation. His ways are higher than our ways. He is the righteous Judge of the universe.

I was instructed to repent for the sins of my ancestors, and I immediately did so. I spoke out every sin that I could think of at that time that could have possibly been committed by either group: murder, jealousy, hatred, envy, treachery, debauchery, treason, malice, greed, sins of omission, sexual perversion, adultery, drunkenness, substance abuse, lying, cheating, conniving, laziness, enmity against almighty God, violence, bloodlust, failure to provide for family and children, failure to steward possessions, family, and finances, witchcraft, sins of the tongue, blasphemy, and profanity.

When I was satisfied that I had successfully confessed my ancestors' sins, I began to ask the Lord to forgive them for their transgressions, wipe away their sins, and remember them no more.

I saw that their bad things were in my blood—and the good things were too. I asked to Lord to "clear and clean my blood" of all these bad things, to filter my blood and cleanse it, and to shine the healing glory light of his precious Son on my blood to make me clean.

As it was being reintroduced into my body, I saw the filters and the fount where the two bloodlines came together. They were being bathed in the glory light of Christ. I knew I was receiving a "holy blood transfusion." All the negative elements in my blood were being removed.

At that point, I knew it was time to claim all the positive and retain it. I began to ask the Lord to bless me down to the thousandth generation for all the prayers of the godly ancestors in my two bloodlines. That is his Word, and I did hold onto it:

> Know therefore that the Lord thy God, he is God, he is the faithful God who keepeth covenant and mercy with them that love him and keep his commandments to a thousand generations. (Deuteronomy 7:9)

This is the path, walk in it.

The Testimony

In the days after having the vision, the Lord began to impress upon me that this was not going to be as simple as just praying, "I confess all my sins and the sins of my ancestors." I wish it were that easy, but that is just not going to do it. I also was reminded of a time back in the early 1990s when I went to a seminar taught by a famous evangelist on the "breaking of generational curses." it was an all-day teaching, and they touted it as a "fix all" for all the generational curses that were in our lives. Well, when the day was over, they told all of us that we were now free from any of the effects of these curses. I remember thinking that I could not have spent my time better than this. Now I was free—or so they said. In the days, weeks, and years after this, I began to realize the truth was that I was *not* free.

Now here I was—some thirty years later but thirty years wiser—having to face the same giant again, the one that was not defeated at the seminar back in the 1990s. This time, my "teacher" would be the Holy Spirit and not a man.

I remember getting up to pray, but instead of praying like I thought I was going to do, he started to unload information to me very rapidly. One of the first things I received was the "sin list." At first, I would just use a small scrap of paper and jot down what he said, but then I had to get full-sized sheets because it was an outpouring and not a drip. For many days, it was this way. I got up to pray and received downloads of information instead.

Finally, I started out in my early morning prayer sessions to repent for the sins of my ancestors, using the sin list that I had been given. I actually planned to do a separate repentance for my own sins later and another separate forgiveness effort after that. This was my way. After having that vision, I realized the urgency of what I had been shown. I knew I had better do something.

During my prayer sessions, I found myself repenting for my own sins and my ancestors' sins and forgiving others at the same time. At first, I was not even conscious of it, but then I saw that it was exactly what I was doing. I looked at the sin list and realized it was not just a sin list; it was a sin/forgive list, and I was led to do all three at the same time. This was his way. It is all the same ball of wax. It was all interrelated.

Now that I was doing it his way, I still did not know where to begin. I began with my earliest memories and repented for my sins and my ancestors' sins, and I forgave others for their trespasses against me. I was going along just fine until I was arrested by the Holy Spirit. The Lord came up behind me like a huge wave of the ocean, and I was lifted up. He took over this repentance himself, in his own way, and I was "granted repentance."

When I look back on it now, I realize that I did not know anything more than

I did back in the 1990s. When he was finished with me, I knew that I had been instructed by the Holy Spirit himself. It was only then that he allowed me to pray each morning. He had a very different approach than I did. He led me from place to place in my life in the order that he wanted to deal with me in. He even made me go back over the areas that I had already covered on my own. That was God's way. Let him lead.

He impressed upon me that these were not complicated issues. You do not need a pastor or a counselor. You don't need sessions with practitioners. This was something that every man or woman had to do on their own—in the privacy of their own homes. The instructions he gave me were quite simple. The entire Gospel is not complicated, although there are many people who would argue that it is and that you need a spiritual advisor or a pastor to be a shepherd over your life and guide you through this. In most cases, I have found that very few of them even know. You need not think that any person can teach you what the Holy Ghost will teach you. He will teach you all you need to know. Just ask him.

I began to pray each morning in the manner in which I was led. I made a huge error in that I started to blame my forefathers and those who had trespassed against me for my problems in life. I was brought before the Lord in this rather quickly and in a dramatic fashion.

One morning, I went into the bathroom, took off my robe, and lathered up my face to shave. I was standing at the bathroom sink and looking at myself in the mirror. I was going to shave and then get into the shower, which is what I do every morning.

As soon as I put the razor up to my cheek, for some reason I said, "What if the lights went out right now?" All of a sudden, they did! I was so shocked that I could hardly believe it. The power never went off there unless there was a severe thunderstorm, but that was not the case.

I had a hard time walking out to the living room and getting a flashlight. I brought it back, got into the shower, and rinsed off. I was completely dumbfounded. I spoke those words out loud without even thinking about them. What could that mean?

I was upset about it and found out that a breaker in the outside panel was tripped and would not reset. I needed a new breaker. I could not get one, and I spent three days in the dark! All the food in my freezer was lost. I was angry!

Finally, the electrician replaced the breaker, and the lights came back on. What a relief. Two weeks later, as I was getting ready to shave, I thought, *what if it happened again?* It immediately did—the same way as before—as soon as I touched the razor to my cheek. I struggled with the flashlight for another three days in the dark. I lost all my food again, and I knew that the chance of that happening twice was astronomical.

I rebuked the devil and bound him. I blamed him for this demonic hindrance, but in prayer, I found out that it was a *holy* hindrance.

The Lord was attempting to get my attention. You see, I had been heavily involved with repentance and forgiveness for myself every morning during my prayer time, and in some cases, I blamed others for my problems. He let me know that before I go blaming circumstances, other people, bad luck, poor timing, and generational curses, I need to take a good look at myself in the mirror. The Lord said, "First, take a good, hard look at yourself." It was a very painful lesson to learn, but I did—and I thank God for it. All I had to go through to learn this impressed upon me how vitally important it is.

In my prayer time now, when I feel led to offer forgiveness for some wrong, I say, "What was my part in this, Lord?" In many cases, you will find that you did have some part in it. You need to ask forgiveness for yourself first and then for the offender. Now, instead of blaming others, I search myself first. If I find that I did have a part in it, I ask forgiveness for it. I also forgive myself.

SECTION I

Sin/Forgive List

Introduction

The following list is by no means all-inclusive. There may be instances and experiences in your own life and the lives of your ancestors that you will need to document and add to this list. Ask the Lord to show you the hidden and unknown things in your life—and in your ancestors' lives—and reveal to you all you need to know.

Start by dealing with the things you do know, and the Lord will pick it up from there. He will begin to guide you. He will actually lead you in the sequence that you must follow. You will undoubtedly know when he has taken over. When he intervened in my repentance, I felt as though a wave in the ocean had picked me up from behind. That is when I knew without a doubt that I had been granted repentance. You see, the Lord's people are "granted repentance," but not everyone else is. What a joy to know that you have gotten the attention of the Lord himself. Let him lead, and he will not go in an orderly fashion, in the way that you, as a human being, understand it. He will jump from here to there, and it may not make sense to you at first, but nevertheless, it is his way—and his ways are far above our ways. Just go with it!

You will notice how the sins you are repenting for on your ancestors' behalf may be the same sins that you are personally guilty of. The first thing I did was repent personally for any of the sins on this list that I felt I may have been guilty of, and then I repented for those exact same sins for my ancestors. Essentially, you will be performing a very detailed and thorough repentance for your own sins at the same time you are repenting for theirs. You will be offering forgiveness to those who have trespassed against you, including your forefathers, because your forefathers' sins have negatively affected you. You're taking care of three entirely related, extremely critical matters at once.

Use the list and whatever else you have added to it—and seek the Lord in your quiet time. It is best to do this the first thing in the morning. You must seek him when he can be found. It has been my experience that he can be found early in the morning. Start out at the beginning of the list and don't jump around. Take it to the Lord line by line. When you feel as though you're done for the day, just put it up and start tomorrow where you left off. This is not a quick sprint. Please do not rush through it. The Lord will lead you day by day.

Once you get into it, you will be excited to get up early and continue. You will actually look forward to doing this each morning. Remember that this is not as simple as praying, "I break every generational curse in my life." If you really want to put a stop to these curses, you're going to have to deal with them thoroughly. Just get started and keep going. You will know when you are finished because one morning, you will get up to continue praying, and there will not be anything left to pray about.

Instructions

Remember to start off your first session with praise, worship, and thanksgiving. Talk to Jesus, tell him what you are about to engage in, and ask for his help. With awe, respect, and reverence, assign holy angels to smooth and pave the way for you and to be at your service.

First, you have to set the atmosphere where you are doing this. This is the prayer I use to set the atmosphere—whether it is in your home, office, car, or somewhere else:

> Lord God, if there be any spirits in this place that are evil, I cast you spirits out now in the name of Jesus Christ. I cast you into the pit, and I seal you in with the blood of Jesus. And if there be any spirits in here that just do not belong here, I give you leave and send you spirits to the feet of Jesus for him to do with them as he will. I now release the Holy Spirit into this place instead. I release the sevenfold Spirit of the Lord and helping spirits from you, Lord, as you would assign. Thank you, Lord. Amen.

Now that you are ready to proceed, you will see that the first item on the list is "enmity against almighty God." Now is a good time to open up in prayer and ask the Holy Spirit to show you what to add to this list that is particular to your own life. Read the list and pray. He will show you anything that you need to pencil in.

Read the overview of enmity against almighty God first, in section II, before starting on the sin/forgive list to get an idea of just what to expect in your pursuit of repentance regarding this category.

Do this with each one of them. Read the overview of the particular category and then proceed with each item on the list. Go through the list methodically.

Step 1
Confess your sins, repent, and ask forgiveness for your transgression against the Lord. Ask him to show you where you have sinned, ask him to forgive you, and then forgive yourself.

Step 2
Repent for the sins of your forefathers. Ask the Lord to show you every instance in which they sinned against him. Confess their transgressions and repent for them.

Step 3

Forgive your ancestors for the harm they have caused you and your descendants. Now forgive all who have harmed you in regard to the first item on the list. Proceed to item 2 on the list, repeat until you are finished with this category, and make notes as you go.

May the Lord be with you and reveal to you everything that you need to know. May he grant you repentance as well as your ancestors. May your blood be cleansed and cleared of all sins. May your forgiven sins and the forgiven sins of your ancestors not affect you or anyone else in your entire line of descendants. I pray this in the name of Jesus Christ. Amen.

Sins of Our Ancestors and Ourselves

Enmity against Almighty God

condition of hatred and animosity against God
blaming God for everything that goes wrong
anger and disappointment with God
mocking God and his Word
denying the existence of God
denying that Jesus is the Son of God
blaspheming God and his Word
atheism

Medical/Dental

medical malpractice and gross negligence
grave mistakes and cover-ups
medical greed
medical disregard of certain persons (no insurance, too old, no money, etc.)
respecters and judges of persons
posing as a doctor or posing as certified in a field
omission of procedure
withholding of care
substandard cleanliness
medical contempt of certain people
incompetence
fraud
lies and deceit
carelessness
haphazard behavior
prescribers of unneeded or even harmful medications
pattern of wrong diagnosis
unwillingness to spend necessary time with patient
snap diagnosis
uncaring/cold

Legal Misrepresentation

courtroom disasters and losses
preponderance of lawsuits against you
attorney malpractice concerning their clients
legal disregard of certain persons whether attorney or judicial
taking bribes to pervert justice whether attorney or judicial
disregard for the pursuit of justice
influence peddling and good old boy's network
not putting in the time or effort required to obtain justice
uncaring and cold
greed
attorney dishonesty
outright fraud
lying to clients
courtroom lies and deceptions

Religious Deception

display of fraudulent anointing
fraudulent revelations and lies
false prophecies
giving of a word falsely
lies and deceit
acting like they have heard from the Lord
seeking the praise of others by deceitful practices
acting reverent and holy
false tongues
creating the illusion of being a man or woman of God
creating the illusion of being a prophet
false claims of healing and deliverance

Theft

shoplifting
stealing from employer
stealing from others
cheating on tax returns

cheating to obtain government benefits
stealing care from others
failure to provide
failure to give time/finances to the Lord
lying to obtain personal gain
conning others for personal gain
defrauding others
trickery
receiving stolen property
misappropriations
embezzlement, extortion, and blackmail

Sins against the Self

being your own worst enemy
misplaced trust
giving unmerited trust
giving of finances without consulting the Lord
futile hope
believing lies
too quick to give of time or funds
making oneself a victim of those seeking to take advantage
self-sabotage
false hope
self-inflicted curses
self-denial
self-inflicted punishments
self-inflicted abstinence
denial of enjoyments
negative testimony of oneself
diminished opinion/consideration of oneself
helping those who you are not supposed to help

Occult Practices

witchcraft
fortune-telling

soothsaying
card reading
palm reading
Ouija boards
sorcery
black magic
freemasonry
secret societies
Luciferianism
demon worship
satanic rituals
worshiping Satan
false religions
occult books, magazines, and comic books
occult games, including children's games and video games
watching occult movies
Halloween

Sexual Sin

unfaithfulness
adultery
homosexuality
perversion
incest
vileness
pornography
fornication
lust
debauchery
lewdness
filthiness
pedophilia
infidelity

Vices

alcoholism
drug abuse
tobacco use
prostitutes
slothfulness
gambling
all sexual sins
stealing
pride
gluttony, food
envy
greed
living in filth
omission of hygiene
hedonism, pleasure seekers
sexual gluttony
gluttony for power
gluttony for other's praise
gluttony for other's approval
gluttony for gathering and gain

Betrayal, Backstabbing, Treachery, and Sabotage

poisoners
cutthroats
betrayers
saboteurs
undercutters
deceivers
con artists
those who plot catastrophes
those who set people up
entrapment
false incrimination
establishing lies as truth
setting people up to fail

arrangers of false or dangerous situations
ruthless people
vicious people
cruel or unprincipled people
willing victim spirit
acting the fool
predatory spirit
professional users
those whose business is tampering with others
those whose entertainment is tampering with others

Murder and Suicide

murder
those who commit suicide
those who push others to commit suicide
those who influence others to commit murder
manslaughter
violence
viciousness
bloodlust
abortion
meanness
coldness
harshness
immorality
criminality

Sins of the Tongue

words of idleness
words of foolishness
words that are faithless
words that agree with the enemy
words that are untrue
words that are profane
words that are blasphemous

words that are unbecoming of the speaker
words that are disparaging to the speaker
any and all other words that are displeasing to the Lord

Insanity

yielding to the spirit of insanity
mental illness in your bloodline
bipolarity
schizophrenia
obsessive-compulsive disorder
sociopathy
psychopathy
narcissism
selfishness
cold, unloving behavior
criminal insanity

Sins Regarding Food

using food to manipulate others
using food as a weapon
purposely contaminating food
gluttony
anorexia
preparing food in unsanitary conditions
having a paranoia of getting spoiled or contaminated food
unnecessary frugality in regard to food
uncaring attitude toward other people's food
eating at questionable establishments
food that is used to curse or cast spells
placing or disguising unholy items in someone else's food (witchcraft)
compromising or adulterating food in order to gain financially
not adhering to "when in doubt, throw it out"
allowing others to present you with questionable food
adulteration/stretching of food
using questionable or unhealthy additives

not serving fresh food
serving food that is too old
serving food that is spoiled
spicing up old or spoiled food to mask it

Accusations

accusing others to a fault
accusing others to police, FBI, CIA, or adult or child protective agencies
accusing others to parents, teachers, spouses, or friends
making false accusations
accusing others to anyone who will listen, even strangers
lying and slandering behind one's back
dropping hints, innuendos, or insinuations
making accusations to color other's opinions in a negative manner
malicious attempts to undermine socially or destroy a person's character
starting or perpetuating smear campaigns
engaging in wholesale slander campaigns
telling big lies mixed with some truth
professional accusers
establishing lies as truth
servants of Satan (witchcraft)
fake recordings
fake videos
fake paperwork
fake records, letters, or affidavits

Financial Damnation or Reversal of Fortune

acceptance of poverty and lack
poor timing
bad luck
poor choices
bad judgment
multiple business failures
recurring patterns
repeated devouring of finances

enemies working against you in the shadows
curses being cast at you
being cursed with automatic failure
attracting buzzards
sabotage
cutthroats
predatory lenders
predatory business associates
professional users
servants of Satan working against you (witchcraft)
bankruptcy

Unlucky in Love / Multiple Marriages

taking a chance
inappropriate choices
mind blinding
mind fog
mind hindering and blocking
letting others push you
rushing in
disregarding reality
not taking it to the Lord
not waiting on the Lord
overlooking the Lord's advice
not hearing from the Lord but taking it as a yes
putting your own wants, needs, and desires ahead of the Lord's plans
succumbing to manipulation
victim of witchcraft

Psychological Abuse

master manipulators
con artists
those who set up others
accusers
tricksters

connivers
deceivers
instigators
craftiness of an evil nature
mind games
emotional blackmail
undue influence
idolaters
controllers
curses and spells from the servants of Satan
sowers of doubt and unbelief
sowers of confusion
purposely offering bad advice
tampering with others
emotional manipulators
compulsive liars
professional users

Sickness, Disease, and Poor Health

chronic diseases
repeated illnesses
failure to steward one's health
taking risks with one's health
sexual sins against one's own body
failure to properly attend to those who are ill
intentionally causing illness or disease
failure to properly exercise
giving or receiving improper medical care
lack of hygiene
straight-out lies of medical professionals
failure to properly treat your own health problems
patterns of health breakdowns
timing of health problems (certain times of the year)
gluttony
anorexia
curses and spells from the servants of Satan

SECTION II

Subject Overview

Enmity against Almighty God

hatred and animosity against God
blaming God for everything that goes wrong
anger and disappointment with God
mocking God and his Word
denying the existence of God
denying that Jesus is the Son of God
blaspheming God and his Word
atheism

Overview

If you are in a condition of hatred and animosity toward almighty God, you are quickly moving beyond your last hope. Many people are disappointed or angry with God, and if you are one of them, I suggest looking inwardly at yourself first. This is not God's fault. After all, he is God. It makes absolutely no sense that it is his fault.

If you have been walking outside of the covenant, not hearing and listening to him, and not bothering to keep his commandments, you are opening the door to problems. If you go one step further and begin to develop a hatred of God and a disdain for his statutes, you will open the door to the demonic. Believe me, friend, that is a door that you do not want to open.

It is not enough to just believe in God and Jesus or even go to church and expect that will be enough to get you into heaven. The scriptures say, "As many as hear my voice and keep my commandments." If that is not you, then what right do you have to the promises of God? I have had problems of that nature myself. I thought I was entitled to all the promises of God when I was clearly not! It wasn't until I started to keep *all* his statutes that I began to be a child of God, and I beheld that each and every promise in that Bible did hold true for me.

It wasn't some complicated theory or complicated, fancy prayers that changed this in my life; it was the attention given to the Lord and praise and worship and the keeping of all his statutes. It is that simple. I had a prophetic dream one night long ago, and in this dream, I found myself standing alone on a pedestal with my arms outstretched to the Lord. I heard in my spirit, "Seek ye first the kingdom of God and his righteousness and all these things will be added to you" (Matthew 6:33). Before you grab your first cup of coffee or check your cell phone, you need to "tithe" the "first fruits" of your day to the Lord. That is the first hours of your day.

I sought his righteousness, and I tithed and hour and a half each day (10 percent of my waking hours), and I have not missed a day since. You have to draw close to him, and he will draw closer to you. I had to build up to it little by little. At first, I was unable to spend one and a half hours with the Lord, but I quickly got there. Don't be dismayed—just keep going.

That is the remedy for all the things you have been missing from the Lord. It's that simple. Go over the list. Not everything on that list applies to you, but everything on that list applies to the generational curses and your forgiveness of others.

Remember step 1, 2, and 3 from the instructions.

Notes

_____

_____

_____

_____

_____

_____

_____

_____

_____

_____

_____

_____

_____

_____

_____

_____

_____

_____

_____

_____

_____

_____

_____

_____

_____

_____

_____

_____

_____

_____

_____

_____

_____

_____

_____

Medical/Dental

medical malpractice and gross negligence

grave mistakes and cover-ups

medical greed

medical disregard of certain persons (no insurance, too old, no money, etc.)

respecters and judges of persons

posing as a doctor or posing as certified in a field

omission of procedure

withholding of care

substandard cleanliness

medical contempt of certain people

incompetence

fraud

lies and deceit

carelessness

haphazard behavior

prescribers of unneeded or even harmful medications

pattern of wrong diagnosis

unwillingness to spend necessary time with patient

snap diagnosis

uncaring/cold

Overview

If you have experienced a high level of this in your life—or the lives of your children and grandchildren—there is a very good chance that this was all brought in by ancestral demons and familiar spirit demons. Somehow, it had the right to afflict you and yours. That right to harm was legally given due to the sins in your inherited bloodline. You may have never committed any of these sins yourself, but if your ancestors did, you will be held responsible as well. Do you see how important it is to follow through and put a stop to this now? You actually have the power in Christ to end this affliction.

Go through the list and whatever you may have added to it, and one by one, ask the Lord to reveal to you just what transpired in the lives of your forefathers that would bring this kind of affliction into your life. Don't just read them off; take your time and give the Holy Spirit space to work. We are on his schedule—not our own. This takes time. Don't rush it. After you ask him, be quiet before the Lord and wait upon him. He will reveal to you the things you need to know.

While you are on each line item in this category, ask the Lord to reveal to you who you need to forgive. Who has wronged you or a loved one in this area? Remember to repent and ask for forgiveness at the same time. If you have sinned in this area, ask the Lord to forgive you and be sure to forgive yourself too. Do not move to the next item on the medical/dental list until you have completed all three steps: your personal repentance, the repentance for your ancestors, and the forgiveness of those who have harmed you regarding this particular item on the list. Pray for the forgiveness of your ancestors for the harm they have caused to you and yours regarding this list.

I have had problems in this area. I had no sin of this kind because I have never been in the medical or dental field. The Lord revealed to me that I had a rich ancestral history of medical and dental forefathers. When I started to go through this list, I began to receive the revelation of just what sins my ancestors had committed, and they had affected me deeply. Once I was finished with this list, I realized the reason for each and every one of my problems. I was able to draw a line to connect each one of them. They were divine revelations.

Notes

Legal Misrepresentation

courtroom disasters and losses
preponderance of lawsuits against you
attorney malpractice concerning their clients
legal disregard of certain persons whether attorney or judicial
taking bribes to pervert justice whether attorney or judicial
disregard for the pursuit of justice
influence peddling and good old boy's network
not putting in the time or effort required to obtain justice
uncaring and cold
greed
attorney dishonesty
outright fraud
lying to clients
courtroom lies and deceptions

Overview

Constant legal problems are also a part of this package. If there is no sin on your part and you are experiencing problems in this area, you may be a victim of ancestral sin through your bloodline. This has to be broken off because you could actually spend the rest of your life fighting losing battles in court and being harassed by lawsuits and accusations. Does justice seem to evade you? Have you had a preponderance of lawsuits against you?

You probably know the history of your parents and grandparents, but how many of us really know anything much past that? Remember to use the list and whatever you have added to it to take to the Lord and ask him to reveal to you the reason that you are experiencing problems in this area. Take your time. Wait on the Lord, and he will show you many things that you did not know. As these things are being revealed to you, you must repent for those sins of your ancestors. Ask the Lord to forgive your forefathers for committing these sins and clear and clean your blood of these sins.

Do you have an excessive repeat of, for example, hiring lawyers—and they do not seem to care about you or justice? Do they keep backing up and never getting anywhere? In the end, do they lose? If they lose, you lose. Look at the list and apply any that fit your situation.

Could it be that they had a certain disregard for you—your financial status, your age, your race, or whatever it was that they did not seem to even have respect for you—even though you were paying them. There is a root cause to this disregard and disrespect, and you will find it in your bloodline. This is a huge gift from the Lord. Use it!

If you have any sins in this area, you need to repent for them now and ask the Lord to forgive you for them. You also need to forgive yourself for those sins and ask that they all be washed away in the blood of his precious Son, Jesus Christ, never to be remembered against you again.

Forgive those who have harmed you or your loved ones in this area. Take your time to let the Lord reveal to you the people who you need to forgive and then forgive them all, one by one. Move on to the next line item on the list under this heading and repeat the process. Repent for your sins and your ancestors' sins—and forgive those who have sinned against you.

Notes

_____

_____

_____

_____

_____

_____

_____

_____

_____

_____

_____

_____

_____

_____

_____

_____

_____

_____

_____

_____

_____

_____

_____

_____

_____

_____

_____

_____

_____

_____

_____

_____

_____

_____

_____

_____

_____

Religious Deception

display of fraudulent anointing
fraudulent revelations and lies
false prophecies
giving of a word falsely
lies and deceit
acting like they have heard from the Lord
seeking the praise of others by deceitful practices
acting reverent and holy
false tongues
creating the illusion of being a man or woman of God
creating the illusion of being a prophet
false claims of healing and deliverance

Overview

This category of ancestral sins is very disturbing in that the very people carrying it out are without the fear of the Lord. How can they use his name and put it to a falsehood? What do they seek? Is it the compliments of others? An elevation or more respect? Can you imagine the Lord at the final judgment asking you to explain this to him? Would you be comfortable carrying this enormous sin and passing it on to your descendants to the third and fourth generations?

What about the scriptures that discuss deceiving and being deceived? If you deceive people in this manner, you will be deceived. If you are deceived, even greatly deceived, you won't even know it! Perhaps this sin was present in your ancestry. If so, it's time to put a stop to it. Don't let it go on through you and past you into your progeny. Believe me, they do not need to inherit this.

It is wise to pay attention to this group of sins in your life and the lives of your ancestors. Look back through your life and ask the Holy Spirit to show you any occasions that you may have engaged in this type of behavior. What about your parents and grandparents? What do you know about them? Do you think there is anything like that in their makeup?

Become aware of this group of sins. Do you see anything like that in your church or your friends and acquaintances? If you ask the Holy Spirit, he will show you those who practice religious deception. Unfortunately, this is rampant in the church and among the body of Christ. Just because they are in a church—or even your church—do not automatically give them your trust. This trust would be "unmerited trust." Outside of your church or ministry, you would not just trust anybody, would you? Put the same filters on the body of Christ—if not more so. Some people seek out church people because they assume that you will automatically trust them. Don't do it!

Take the so-called prophets of today, including the famous and the relatively unknown local prophets. Don't just take a word from them without using your discernment to weigh it. The Holy Spirit will give you the discernment to distinguish between the real Word of God and a false word. If someone gives me a prophecy or a word, I immediately know if it is of God or not. I had to practice and go to the Lord when I wasn't sure. Now I know while I am receiving these unsolicited gifts—whether they are true and of God or not. I do not have to go home and ponder it anymore and pray about it because I already know. You will get there too, my dear friend. You have to because so much depends upon it.

Notes

Theft

shoplifting
stealing from employer
stealing from others
cheating on tax returns
cheating to obtain government benefits
stealing care from others
failure to provide
failure to give time/finances to the Lord
lying to obtain personal gain
conning others for personal gain
defrauding others
trickery
receiving stolen property
misappropriations
embezzlement, extortion, and blackmail

Overview

If you have been the victim of theft, which can show a pattern of being susceptible to thefts of any kind or even all kinds, then you may have this trait in your bloodline. Remember to look at your own life first. Are you honest and forthright? Sometimes it can be a little of you and your bloodline combined; after all, if this is in your bloodline, it will tend to bend or twist you in that direction as well. That is the nature of generational curses Remember the old saying about like father, like son? The blood of your ancestors will undoubtedly affect you in this manner. Know this.

You have to look at your parents and grandparents—and your aunts, uncles, cousins, children, and grandchildren. If you look at the lives of any of these blood relatives, and you will see a common denominator. Look separately at each of your two bloodlines to see the patterns. Ask the Lord to expand on this during your prayer time and shine his light on the hidden and unknown things. He will reveal to you all that you need to know. Once I did this, I began to see where all this came in to me. I made a list of my father's bloodline and my mother's bloodline. I listed everything I had learned, and I contemplated it with the Lord in prayer. He opened up the truth to me.

You must repent for their sins—as well as your own. Ask the Lord to forgive them—and you—for these trespasses. Ask him to clear and clean your blood of these transgressions and then forgive all who have trespassed against you in this area.

Notes

Sins against the Self

being your own worst enemy

misplaced trust

giving unmerited trust

giving of finances without consulting the Lord

futile hope

believing lies

too quick to give of time or funds

making oneself a victim of those seeking to take advantage

self-sabotage

false hope

self-inflicted curses

self-denial

self-inflicted punishments

self-inflicted abstinence

denial of enjoyments

negative testimony of oneself

diminished opinion/consideration of oneself

helping those who you are not supposed to help

Overview

This is a very long list, unfortunately, and it has very harmful and long-lasting effects, some of which you may have actually brought on yourself, either unknowingly or through ignorance. The enemy can look at what has happened to you and say, "I had nothing to do with this. This is a matter of their testimony about themselves." The devil is quite capable of causing harm without your help. Don't help him—fight him. Your life depends on it.

Some people are their own worst enemies. You may have seen this on display in people in your life. Maybe it is a part of your life as well. If it is, it ends here, my friend. Just keep reading and learning.

I have known people who endure self-inflicted punishments, unnecessary abstinence, or self-denial of enjoyment. You need to be your own best friend first!

Watch your tongue! It has the power of life and death in it, and you will eat the fruit of what you say. Never say anything negative about yourself, your children, or your grandchildren. These will turn into self-inflicted curses that you have proclaimed out of your very own mouth. Nobody has more authority than you to curse yourself or your bloodline. Drop all negative testimony of yourself and your bloodline. Words have power. Many people do not realize that, but since you do, you should act accordingly.

You cannot do it on your own, but with God, all things are possible. You can start today and ask the Lord to forgive you for the sins of your tongue. Pray that this behavior stops; this type of thing could be very well ingrained in you and your ancestors. What things have you heard your parents say in ignorance? What have you said about yourself and to your children in ignorance? It is extremely important to cleanse your tongue. (A prayer is offered later in this book.)

When you look deeper into these things in your prayer time, you will realize that this isn't just you; it is an inherited trait. Who else in your family is or was prone to this behavior? Was it on both sides of the family or just one? You have to forgive yourself for any of this and forgive your ancestors as well. You need to break the power of the ancestral curses and ask to be released from the effects and consequences of these sins. Forgive all those who have harmed you or your loved ones in this area.

Notes

Occult Practices

witchcraft
fortune-telling
soothsaying
card reading
palm reading
Ouija boards
sorcery
black magic
freemasonry
secret societies
Luciferianism
demon worship
satanic rituals
worshiping Satan
false religions
occult books, magazines, and comic books
occult games, including children's games and video games
watching occult movies
Halloween

Overview

This is extremely serious and damaging to yourself and your descendants. The Bible warns us to stay away from all forms of the occult. The occult is Satan's exclusive domain. If you dabble in this, neither you nor your descendants will go unscathed. You probably know to stay away from witchcraft, sorcery, and black magic, and you probably would never go to satanic rituals or worship demons, but did you know that there is a list of more subtle practices that also need to be avoided? Here are some of them—yoga, Zen, any of the Eastern religions, freemasonry, secret societies, and cults—just to name a few. If you have any occult games or children's games, books, magazines, or occult comic books, get rid of them. If you watch occult movies on television, you need to stop. These things have been normalized by society, but they are actually dangerous. Some of them are designed to cast spells. Are you aware that many of today's musicians are into the occult? Have you noticed the "signs" they throw up? These include devil horns, pyramid signs, 666 signs, and covering one eye to signal the all-seeing eye? They are even bold enough to throw it right in your face repeatedly because it enhances their power and you might not even notice it. The same holds true for actors and actresses. Look at some of the magazine covers. How many of them picture an artist with one hand covering an eye? Why are they all doing that? What about the finger over the lips? How many magazine covers have that image on them? You need to be aware of this and act accordingly.

If you celebrate Halloween, you need to stop. This is not an innocent holiday. It is actually one of the high holy days of the occult, and it requires a blood sacrifice. Witches have said, "Thank you, Christians. This is the one holiday on our calendar that we can count on you to help us celebrate."

Go over the list, and if you have been involved in any of this, you need to renounce your involvement and ask forgiveness for yourself as well as your ancestors.

Bring up each item on the list to the Lord in your prayer time and ask him to show you where this occurred in your ancestry. Forgive your ancestors and ask the Lord to clear and clean your blood of any and all involvement in the occult.

If you are guilty of any of these sins, you must repent for each and every one of them. Reference the list and anything that you have penciled in. Take your time, let the Lord reveal to you everything—even things you have forgotten—and ask for his forgiveness.

Forgive everyone who has sinned against you in this area, including your ancestors, and ask the Lord to reveal them to you. I did this, and I was amazed at what was revealed to me.

Notes

Sexual Sin

unfaithfulness
adultery
homosexuality
perversion
incest
vileness
pornography
fornication
lust
debauchery
lewdness
filthiness
pedophilia
infidelity

Overview

Many of us have had problems in this area—just as our ancestors did on each side of our bloodlines. This has to be brought before the Lord and repented for. Start with the first item and repent for your sins if applicable. Move into repentance for your ancestors and then into forgiveness of others regarding this item. Move down to the next item on the list and repeat. Do this until you reach the end of the list—along with anything you have added to it.

The key is to repent and ask forgiveness for yourself and for each one of your ancestors who may have been guilty of any of these sins. Ask the Lord to wash you and them in the blood of his precious Son, Jesus Christ, and wash away those sins, never to be remembered against you again. Ask that you will not be held accountable for them at the final judgment because they just do not exist anymore—even now.

Give time to the Holy Spirit to reveal things to you. It does not happen right away; in most cases, you have to ask and wait upon him.

This is not something that you can move through quickly.

Notes

Vices

alcoholism
drug abuse
tobacco use
prostitutes
slothfulness
gambling
all sexual sins
stealing
pride
gluttony, food
envy
greed
living in filth
omission of hygiene
hedonism, pleasure seekers
sexual gluttony
gluttony for power
gluttony for other's praise
gluttony for other's approval
gluttony for gathering and gain

Overview

The vices are many, and they comprise a long list. Add to this list as you feel led to. When I mention vices to people, they seem to equate them to alcohol, tobacco, drug use, and gambling, but the list is much longer than that. I've known people who have a food vice. They feel a need to consume way too much of it, which is gluttony. There are also shopping vices, sexual vices, and people who are ensnared by power. Some people crave praise or approval and are gluttons for gathering and gain. They just can't seem to get enough money, property, or valuables. They are consumed by greed.

If any of this pertains to you, it probably came from one or both of your bloodlines. If that is so, you will be prone to the same sins. You will be bent or twisted to these same sins—and you will attract people who are similarly stained. This needs to be dealt with and broken. The prayers in this book will help you and your descendants break free.

You don't have to carry this with you any longer. The first step, of course, is to start with the first item on the list and repent for your own sins, if any, pertaining to that item. Ask the Lord to reveal anything that you need to know.

Go into ancestral repentance for the first item. This may take longer because you are dealing with many people instead of just you. Ask the Lord to reveal and expose your ancestral bloodline in regard to the first item. Repent for them in earnest.

The third step is to forgive others who were ensnared by vices that inflicted harm upon you. Take your time and ask the Lord to reveal every person who hurt you because of their bondage to a vice or vices. You don't have to depend on your own memory because the Holy Spirit will bring to mind every episode. However, you have to ask him. Remember to include your ancestors on both sides for the harm they have passed down to you, your children, and your grandchildren.

Notes

Betrayal, Backstabbing, Treachery, and Sabotage

poisoners
cutthroats
betrayers
saboteurs
undercutters
deceivers
con artists
those who plot catastrophes
those who set people up
entrapment
false incrimination
establishing lies as truth
setting people up to fail
arrangers of false or dangerous situations
ruthless people
vicious people
cruel or unprincipled people
willing victim spirit
acting the fool
predatory spirit
professional users
those whose business is tampering with others
those whose entertainment is tampering with others

Overview

Backstabbing, betrayal, treachery, and sabotage definitely run in family bloodlines. Much destruction within the family, the workplace, and the community can be attributed to these demonic practices. You see the very nature of Satan expressed. He is here to kill, steal, and destroy, and his servants are like him. Many times, the perpetrators seek the help of witches and Satanists to help them destroy because they are totally obsessed with the need to carry out these deeds. If left unchecked, they will leave a path of destruction in their wake ten miles wide and a hundred miles long.

Instead of holding up their families, workplaces, and communities, they are working to destroy those godly institutions. Don't for one minute think that everybody is pretty much the same just because we are all human beings. We are not the same! The people who behave in this manner are doing the work of Satan, and in most cases, they are doing it just to do it and not for gain.

If you have had repeated problems in your life with betrayal, backstabbing, treachery, or sabotage, they can become hallmarks that actually define your life. You may have these problems somewhere in your bloodline—quite possibly on both sides. Go over the list and cover each and every item thoroughly in prayer.

If these are in your bloodline, you may be similarly colored—so be very careful when repenting for yourself. Don't just dismiss it as not applicable. The good news is that even if there is a pattern of this in your life, you may not possess the slightest leaning toward it at all! Trust the Lord to lead you. Do not try to take charge yourself. In my experience, if you try to take charge, he will back off and let you, saying, "OK, you want to handle this on your own? Go right ahead." Believe me, you do not want to handle this or any of this repentance or forgiveness on your own. You would be wasting your time at best, and you may cause serious damage at worst. My best advice is to wait upon him and let him lead you.

Repent for anything that you may be guilty of—item by item—and repent for the sins of your ancestors—item by item. Forgive those who have perpetrated these sins upon you—item by item.

Notes

Murder and Suicide

murder
those who commit suicide
those who push others to commit suicide
those who influence others to commit murder
manslaughter
violence
viciousness
bloodlust
abortion
meanness
coldness
harshness
immorality
criminality

Overview

This category is sometimes presented as a pattern in the lives of family members. If there have been suicides or murders in your family—and this includes your extended family, including everyone you know of and have heard of, your ancestors, and your living relatives—you need to take your time and put an end to it now. I'm talking about an abnormal incidence of these things.

Pray about each one of the items on the list and ask the Lord to show you what you need to repent of and what you need to repent of for your ancestors. Who do you need to forgive? You are going to have to give them a gift that they certainly do not deserve with your forgiveness. Do it by an act of your will. Ask the Lord to give you the grace to forgive them with the same grace by which you were forgiven.

This is something that must end with you. You are the one who has been chosen by the Lord to end this now so that it does not follow your children and grandchildren. Ask the Lord to clear and clean your blood from the effects and consequences of your sins and of the sins of your ancestors. God abhors the shedding of innocent blood.

Are you aware that abortion is also the shedding of innocent blood? If you have been involved with abortion—either as a mother or father or by working in an abortion clinic, including anything at all to do with abortion—you will be held accountable for these sins at the final judgment. The good news is that you can repent for these sins and ask to be forgiven. He is faithful and true to wash away those sins in the blood of his precious Son, Jesus Christ. They will never be held against you again—and you will not be held accountable for them at the final judgment because they simply do not exist anymore, even now.

Notes

Sins of the Tongue

words of idleness
words of foolishness
words that are faithless
words that agree with the enemy
words that are untrue
words that are profane
words that are blasphemous
words that are unbecoming of the speaker
words that are disparaging to the speaker
any and all other words that are displeasing to the Lord

Overview

Have you had problems with controlling your words? Have you prayed and prayed about it and not seemed to make much progress? There may be contamination in one or both of your bloodlines. Once I addressed this in my own life, my words began to line up with the Word of God. I became acutely aware of every word I spoke, each and every day. (I have left you a prayer here, the one that God gave me to use, to keep you aware and forgiven.)

Be very careful what words you use with your children. You, as the parent, have authority over them to bless them or curse them. Every time that you get angry with them, be very careful about what you say to them. Never use disparaging words with them. You cannot say, "You're so dumb. How could you get a D in this subject? How dumb can you be?" I don't have to list other examples for you. You already know them. Each and every time you use words like that to your children, you are cursing them— and you are not even aware of it! Instead, try to say, "Well, I see you received a D in this subject, and now we know what we have to work on. You are much smarter than that." Praise them and tell them how blessed you are to have them as your child. Tell them how brilliant they are. You get the picture, don't you? Using disparaging language with your own children is damaging them, and it has to stop right away.

Be very careful about the words you use to describe yourself. Never use disparaging words or negative words. Don't say, "That's just my luck," "This always happens to me," "I can't do anything right," "It's just me," or "It's only me." Never use words that are unbecoming to the man or woman of God who you are. Speak like the child of God who you truly are. Watch your words so that absolutely none of them are displeasing unto God.

Never agree with the enemy. Other people, although innocently, will sometimes say things to you that you should not agree to. I have found this to be a subtle snare in my life. I had a doctor say, "Well, you know, you have this disease, and it's eventually going to kill you."

I said, "Yes, I know, but I'm doing the best I can." By the time I got out into the parking lot, I was convicted for agreeing with the enemy. (Not that the doctor was an enemy.) I had to start repenting for that right away. What a horrible thing for me to agree to! As it turned out, upon further testing by a different doctor, I did not even have that disease! I didn't find that out for more than two years. Never agree with anyone who goes against the knowledge of the Most High God. (There will be another book that goes into greater detail on this subject at a later date.)

For now, be very aware of your words. Repent for any words that are not right in the Father's eyes. Renounce those words. Recall those words. Ask the holy angels to go out, gather them up, bring them back, and bury them at the feet of Jesus. Repent for the words of your ancestors on both sides. Ask the Lord to show you their transgressions in their spoken words. He will start opening up to you about what you are genetically made of.

Forgive all others who have spoken words to you that were not correct in the Father's eyes, especially those who were or are in authority over you, including parents, teachers, and supervisors. This will take time because you have undoubtedly endured many instances of ill-spoken words by many people. We all have. This has to be worked through.

Prayer

Now, Father, I confess the sins of my tongue over the past day—or several days. I confess any and all words that I spoke that were words of idleness, words of foolishness, words that were agreeing with the enemy, and words that were faithless, blasphemous, profane, or untrue.

I confess any words that were unbecoming of me or even disparaging to me and any and all other words that were displeasing unto you. I confess them now as sin, and I renounce those words. I renounce each and every word that I spoke that was not right in your eyes. I recall those words from floating through the universe, and I send a detail of holy angels out to gather them up in nets and bring them back and bury them at the feet of Jesus.

I ask to be forgiven for those words, and I forgive myself and ask that those unfortunate words be washed away in the blood of your precious Son, Jesus Christ, never to be remembered against me again. I will not have to give an account for those words at the final judgment because they simply do not even exist anymore—even now.

Notes

Insanity

yielding to the spirit of insanity
mental illness in your bloodline
bipolarity
schizophrenia
obsessive-compulsive disorder
sociopathy
psychopathy
narcissism
selfishness
cold, unloving behavior
criminal insanity

Overview

Has there been any insanity in your family that you know of? What about stories of your ancestors who you never met? I hope this bloodline curse is not a part of your makeup, but how many of us even know about our ancestors any further back than two or three generations? It is wise to bring this up to the Lord in your prayer time. Go over the list and anything else that you have added to it. Ask the Lord to show you the sins of your ancestors in this area, and he surely will. Take your time. You are waiting on the Lord—don't ever forget that.

As things are revealed to you, if you have anything in you, repent for yourself first and then for your ancestors. Ask the Lord to forgive you for any transgressions against him and then repent for the transgressions of your ancestors. Many times, these things are inherited—just as physical disease is inherited. I have found that it is most likely to have come from the sins of our forefathers. It has to be stopped from going any further. Repent for these sins on their behalf because they had a beginning—way back somewhere in your bloodline. For example, if your great-grandmother had schizophrenia, and she certainly did not commit any sin to cause her to have that disease, she may have been afflicted with it due to the sins of some of the people in her bloodline. You actually have the authority to break the power of this in your life and in the lives of your progeny. Just do it.

You need to forgive everyone who has damaged you do to the spirit of insanity, including your ancestors. Ask Jesus to reveal every episode of this to you. Forgive them all by an act of your will and ask the Lord to give you the same grace that he used to forgive you so that you may accomplish this.

Notes

Sins Regarding Food

using food to manipulate others
using food as a weapon
purposely contaminating food
gluttony
anorexia
preparing food in unsanitary conditions
having a paranoia of getting spoiled or contaminated food
unnecessary frugality in regard to food
uncaring attitude toward other people's food
eating at questionable establishments
food that is used to curse or cast spells
placing or disguising unholy items in someone else's food (witchcraft)
compromising or adulterating food in order to gain financially
not adhering to "when in doubt, throw it out"
allowing others to present you with questionable food
adulteration/stretching of food
using questionable or unhealthy additives
not serving fresh food
serving food that is too old
serving food that is spoiled
spicing up old or spoiled food to mask it

Overview

Food is sacred unto the Lord, and he does not take lightly any sin regarding the nourishment of his saints. Go over the list and anything you have added to it. Never disregard anything on the list because you do not really know what happened in previous generations. However, you can disregard any item on the list that does not apply to you in your personal repentance.

Again, just ask the Lord to reveal to you any and all transgressions for each item of the list. Wait upon the Lord, and he will reveal things to you at his timing. Do not be in a hurry on this. Just wait.

Of course, using food as a weapon or a controlling tool is part of this repentance—and so is misuse of food, as in gluttony or as a "drug" or release. Food is an enjoyment to be sure, but it was never meant to take the place of Jesus in your life. Be wise in your consumption and your choices. There are many poor choices in the grocery stores—just don't choose them. Invite Jesus into this area of your life. Give him permission to enter this part of your life. This is extremely important. Invite him in. Give him permission. He will redirect things for you, and you will be amazed. I know that I was.

We also have to deal with ancestral sins for the subject of food, including any ancestors who were involved with purposely contaminating food in any way. Poisons, toxins, unsanitary conditions, spoiled food, and uncaring attitudes toward other people's food? Take these one at a time—and repent for any sins that have been revealed to you.

Have any of your ancestors been involved with food manufacturing and processing? Bring that up to the Lord and ask if they crossed any lines in their efforts. I have seen unnecessary additives put in just to fill up the vats and cookers in order to stretch the food out to get as much as possible, depleting the nutrients of each portion. The people were buying the food, but it was not providing them with the nutrients that it was supposed to because it was cut in order to get more. You have to see all the possibilities where sin may have been hiding regarding food.

Acknowledge your sins in this area, repent, and ask the Lord to forgive you. Forgive yourself and ask that these sins all be washed away in the blood of his precious Son, Jesus Christ, never to be remembered against you again. These sins will not be held against you at the final judgment because they do not exist anymore.

Now repent for the sins of your forefathers. Go line by line on the list and seek the Lord's revelation for you regarding their transgressions. Ask him to forgive them—and you must forgive them also.

Forgive all those who have trespassed against you in this area. Ask him to reveal to you the people as well as the food wholesalers, retailers, manufacturers, restaurants, caterers, and anyone or anything else that has ever harmed you regarding food.

Forgive your ancestors for their transgressions regarding food. Forgive them for the damage they have passed down to you through your ancestral bloodlines. The Lord will reveal them to you if you only ask.

Notes

Accusations

accusing others to a fault

accusing others to police, FBI, CIA, or adult or child protective agencies

accusing others to parents, teachers, spouses, or friends

making false accusations

accusing others to anyone who will listen, even strangers

lying and slandering behind one's back

dropping hints, innuendos, or insinuations

making accusations to color other's opinions in a negative manner

malicious attempts to undermine socially or destroy a person's character

starting or perpetuating smear campaigns

engaging in wholesale slander campaigns

telling big lies mixed with some truth

professional accusers

establishing lies as truth

servants of Satan (witchcraft)

fake recordings

fake videos

fake paperwork

fake records, letters, or affidavits

Overview

I have lived long enough to see that some people actually have the nature of Satan himself. They seem to be "professional accusers of the brethern." I have seen people who are obsessed with making false accusations about others to anyone who will listen.

Are there now—or have there been—any false accusers in your life? What about your family and friends? What about relatives you have never met? What about any stories about your ancestors? Go over each item on the list, take it to God, and repent for any sins that you are guilty of first—and then repent for your ancestors. Finally, forgive all those who have damaged you as a result of false accusations. In each instance, you are going to have to go the Lord and ask him for the revelation.

The best accusation—and the one that will stick—is the one that has even a small grain of truth to it. Keep that in mind.

If you have suffered an inordinate amount of vicious false allegations, your ancestors probably engaged in this despicable sin. This sin has destroyed many good people. Go over the list, add to it if you have to, and repent for your ancestors. It's time to put a stop to it. Dwell on this during your prayer time with the Lord. I use this prayer to neutralize these types of threats. It has changed my life because it works. Use it together with the repentance of the sins of your ancestors.

Prayer

Father God, I ask you to put an impenetrable hedge of protection around me today for I have need of it. I ask you for an impenetrable hedge of protection to protect me from the attacks of the enemy, the demonic, the disembodied lost souls, the spiritual wickedness in high places, and the wicked people. I decree that a supernatural coat of resiliency cover me today so that any accusations or negative talk will have to slip right off. Father, I pray that if anyone says anything negative against me in any way or falsely accuses me of any supposed misdeed that no weapon formed against me or us will prosper (Isaiah 54:17). I bind the accuser, and I loose the opposite spirit into my life today. In the name of Jesus, amen.

Notes

Financial Damnation or Reversal of Fortune

acceptance of poverty and lack

poor timing

bad luck

poor choices

bad judgment

multiple business failures

recurring patterns

repeated devouring of finances

enemies working against you in the shadows

curses being cast at you

being cursed with automatic failure

attracting buzzards

sabotage

cutthroats

predatory lenders

predatory business associates

professional users

servants of Satan working against you (witchcraft)

bankruptcy

Overview

Financial damnation, poverty, and lack can come from a number of sources besides generational curses. If this is a factor in your life, it is highly likely that generational curses have played a major part in letting this come to you. There are other factors as well, including your own mistakes and sins.

Look at the list, start with the first item (acceptance of poverty and lack), and ask yourself if this has been a problem in your life. Have you given up and resigned yourself to the status quo? Remember to look at yourself first. Please do not make the same mistake that I did in blaming circumstances, others, poor timing, and generational curses for your problems before you take a good look at yourself. If you ask the Lord, he will show you your part in each and every episode in your life. Acknowledge your part, confess your sin, repent for it, and ask him to forgive you before you go any further.

Go down the list, bring up each item to the Lord, and talk to him about it. He is the only one you can truly trust. Ask him to show you your transgressions and then confess, repent, and forgive yourself. After asking the Lord to show you the generational sins of your forefathers, confess each one—almost as if you were responsible for them yourself—and repent for them in earnest. Forgive your forefathers for the harm they have caused you and your descendants. Forgive all who have harmed you in regard to the first item on the list before going on to the next item.

Be very careful with your words because they have the power to change things for the better or for the worse. Look through Proverbs to see if you are guilty of any infractions against the Lord and yourself. Don't be anxious about anything, especially money, because that can be a snare unto you.

Ask the Lord to forgive you for the damage you have caused to your own progeny. Although it was not intentional, it is still true. Forgive yourself for hurting your progeny. Ask the Lord to reverse the damage you have caused for them. Ask him to clear and clean your blood and their blood so this financial damnation, poverty, and lack are arrested and go no further in your bloodline or the bloodlines of your descendants. Ask him to give all of you a "holy blood transfusion."

May God richly bless you, your descendants, and your loved ones with a double blessing upon you for you have shown the courage to address this and put a stop to it once and for all.

Notes

Unlucky in Love / Multiple Marriages

taking a chance
inappropriate choices
mind blinding
mind fog
mind hindering and blocking
letting others push you
rushing in
disregarding reality
not taking it to the Lord
not waiting on the Lord
overlooking the Lord's advice
not hearing from the Lord but taking it as a yes
putting your own wants, needs, and desires ahead of the Lord's plans
succumbing to manipulation
victim of witchcraft

Overview

Many people have had major problems in this area. They make up all kinds of excuses for them. They say, "My picker is just broken" or "I always seem to attract those kinds of men or women." In a sense, it is actually true. The good news is that it can stop here for you and for your descendants. Imagine your sons and daughters—and their sons and daughters—not having to go through what you went through! You will be able to educate them in what you have learned. Your blood and their blood will be cleaned and cleared of all negative influences—and you all will have been given a holy blood transfusion.

Never take a chance—and don't just dive in and hope for the best. Your adversary, the devil, is roaming about to see who he may devour. If you leave any opening—even one as small as a little crack—he will pry it all the way open and rend you.

Never make a choice that is inappropriate, especially in the vital area of a mate. These choices are called inappropriate because that is exactly what they are. You and your mate will suffer for any poor choices.

Your mind can be fogged up or even blinded by infatuation, lust, convenience, need, or many other things. The enemy can actually block you from perceiving the things that you need to comprehend. In the prayer section of this book, there is a prayer that can prohibit the enemy from doing this (see "Breaking Curses," paragraph 3). I have included these prayers because when you are complete in the personal repentance, forefathers' repentance, and forgiveness, you are going to need them.

Since I started using these prayers, I have actually overcome the enemy. I memorized all of them, and I say them almost every day. Revelation 12:11 tells us that we have overcome the enemy by the blood of the Lamb, the Word of God, and the word of our testimony.

Do not let any others push you—and certainly do not rush in. I have seen parents and well-meaning family members pushing and shoving their children into marriages. This will rarely work out. Follow your own heart—and that the Lord's will be done.

Make sure that you are aware of all the possibilities—and do not overlook the reality that is right in front of you!

Not taking things to the Lord, waiting on the Lord, overlooking the Lord's advice, and not hearing from the Lord and taking it as a yes all have to do with not asking or hearing from the Lord. Take these things to the Lord, ask him, and wait to hear from him. He is not on your schedule or your prospective spouse's schedule, and he is not in a hurry. Let him work.

Do not overlook the Lord's advice. That is actually a very easy thing to do. He will be a still, small voice and not a loud voice. He will attempt to get your attention in many ways—so be watchful for them. You may see and hear his answer in your dreams. When you think, *Oh, that is probably just me,* that should set off an alarm!

If you keep praying and are not getting an answer, do not automatically take it as a yes. Receiving no answer to your prayer is never a yes. You probably have been getting an answer that you may not have liked.

Do not put your own wants, needs, or desires ahead of the Lord's plans for you. If you're doing that, things probably won't turn out well for you. Search yourself, ask him to reveal to you what you need to know, and listen.

If you need to take a time-out, go ahead and take one. Get off your phone and computer and get away to clear your head. After a few days "out of the spin," you will be able to see more clearly. Another advantage of getting away is that once things are quieter, you will be able to hear what the Lord is trying to tell you. Listen. You're not on your own here; the Lord is actually with you!

There is no such thing as "white witchcraft." Anytime a person seeks to control another person, it is witchcraft. Make no mistake about it. I have seen family members of a prospective spouse get together to invoke so-called white witchcraft to secure a desired outcome. I refer you back the prayer section of "Breaking Curses."

You have to take each of these items separately to the Lord:

Step 1
Confess your sins, repent, and ask forgiveness for your transgressions against him. Ask him to show you where you have sinned, ask him to forgive you, and then forgive yourself.

Step 2
Confess the sins of your forefathers and repent for them. Remember to ask him to show you where they have sinned. Ask him to forgive them their trespasses.

Step 3
Forgive your ancestors for the harm they have caused to you and your descendants. Now forgive all who have harmed you in regard to the first item on the list. Proceed to the second item on the list and repeat until you are finished with this category.

Notes

Psychological Abuse

master manipulators
con artists
those who set up others
accusers
tricksters
connivers
deceivers
instigators
craftiness of an evil nature
mind games
emotional blackmail
undue influence
idolaters
controllers
curses and spells from the servants of Satan
sowers of doubt and unbelief
sowers of confusion
purposely offering bad advice
tampering with others
emotional manipulators
compulsive liars
professional users

Overview

Look at this list! If you have suffered a lot of this kind of abuse, then you probably have ancestral sins in this area. Maybe a spouse, friend, or relative played these mind games. If you have been guilty of these despicable practices or are prone or bent toward these sins because they were present in your bloodline, you will definitely attract these types of people into your life. They will add to your pain, and if you have been abused like this, they will spiritually sense a stain or discoloration in you and be magnetically attracted to you because of it.

I have seen this pattern repeated over and over again in many people's lives, and it will keep happening to you and your progeny until it is stopped. Few people realize why this keeps happening to them. This holds true for almost anything negative that just keeps happening over and over again. There is a reason why this has permission to torment you.

The good news is that Jesus Christ has provided a way for you to be free of it and to stop it from going any further in your progeny. So, what are you doing today that could be more important than that? Make time to bring all this to Jesus. Go over the list and add anything that you need to, preferably early in the morning. Talk to him, tell him all about it, and you will find that he is listening to your every word. Recount those episodes to him, and he will show you why these patterns exist. Repent for your sins, one at a time, for each item on the list—and then repent for your forefathers' sins for this same item. Ask the Lord to reveal them to you, forgive all others who have harmed you for this sin, and ask the Lord to bring them to mind—each and every one of them.

Ask the Lord to wash away your sins in the blood of his precious Son, Jesus Christ, never to be remembered against you again. You will not have to give an account of these sins at your final judgment because these sins will no longer exist.

Remember that he is faithful and true to forgive us for our sins. You will start to feel much better after you start unloading these sins. This is actually a huge burden that you need to drop.

Notes

Sickness, Disease, and Poor Health

chronic diseases

repeated illnesses

failure to steward one's health

taking risks with one's health

sexual sins against one's own body

failure to properly attend to those who are ill

intentionally causing illness or disease

failure to properly exercise

giving or receiving improper medical care

lack of hygiene

straight-out lies of medical professionals

failure to properly treat your own health problems

patterns of health breakdowns

timing of health problems (certain times of the year)

gluttony

anorexia

curses and spells from the servants of Satan

Overview

Although many things can cause sickness and disease, one of them is certainly generational curses, especially when it comes to inherited diseases, chronic diseases, and repeated illnesses. You might have to deal with the other causes of disease as well (see section III). One of the possibilities is your own failure to steward your body as the Lord entrusted you to do. You are his guest here on earth, and he has provided this body for your temporary use while you are here. Look at it like that because that is the way it really is. Please do not disrespect this. Poor stewardship will bring about a forfeiture of good health.

A good way to start is to begin to change any poor eating habits or poor lifestyle choices. I don't have to make a list for you because you already know. Clean things up, change things up, and begin the process as you go over the list and repent. See? You have already addressed one major issue.

Go over the list and any other things that you have added to it and repent for your sins, starting with the first item. Ask the Lord to reveal to you the specific episodes in your life where you have transgressed and then go on to the sins of your ancestors regarding the first item. Ask the Lord to show you their transgressions and repent for them as well. The sins of your forefathers will bring about sickness and disease in your life and in the lives of your descendants—just as your own personal sins will. Address each one of them separately and in detail.

Give the Lord the space to reveal to you what he desires to reveal. Never rush it. I have found that you need to wait upon the Lord no matter what. Ask and wait. He will show you what you need to know in his time—not yours. Initially, you may have to wait upon him to respond, but when he does, he will overwhelm you with knowledge. Be ready with pen and paper or a recorder.

When you are finished with this category, you will have covered all the sins that you are guilty of as well as the sins of your ancestors. You will have offered heartfelt repentance for yourself and for your ancestors. This is a major step, and it will have life-changing effects for you and for all your descendants. You could not have given them a greater gift than this. God bless you.

Notes

Congratulations!

Now that you have reached the end of the list, you will have repented thoroughly for your own transgressions against the Lord. These sins have been washed away by the blood of his precious Son, Jesus Christ, never to be remembered against you again. You will not have to give an account for them at your final judgment because they do not exist anymore. Salvation and redemption. You are a clean vessel, and you should keep it that way by repenting as you go, which that is what I do. I don't let more than two or three days go by without repenting for my sins—both known and unknown.

With the repentance for the sins of your forefathers, you will have broken the bonds that have been in place around you and your descendants. You and yours will no longer carry their sins. These burdens will be lifted off of you. The bondage will be broken in Jesus's name.

Forgiving those who have damaged you is a life-changing step. Your life will never be the same. Your descendants' lives will never be the same. You and your children, grandchildren, and great-grandchildren have truly been given a holy blood transfusion.

May God richly bless you and your descendants and loved ones. May he make his face shine upon you and give you grace and peace. May he put his name on all of you. In Jesus's name. Amen.

Seal It with Communion

When you have gone over the entire list and all your additions, you will have reached a point where there is nothing left. When this happened to me, I got up early—just like every other morning—and I took over where I left off. Nothing! I was worried that I was not going to hear from the Lord. I was not doing this repentance on my own. He was leading me, and then he was totally silent—until he pressed upon me that I was finished. I was sort of disappointed because I loved that time with the Lord, and I had accomplished and learned so much. At the same time, I was totally unburdened. I felt so free. The Lord impressed upon me that it was time to seal it with Communion.

I opened my Bible to 1 Corinthians, starting at verse 1, and I gathered the Communion elements and began to pray. I began with praise and thanksgiving because that is the way into his throne room. Never omit that part.

In most churches today, Communion is somewhat of a ritual. The Bible says to do it, so they are, but the manner in which they are doing it is not correct. I have been in many churches where it only took a few minutes to do. Who can commune with the Creator in just a few minutes? I have been in many other churches where they just leave Communion elements on a table for those wishing to participate, and they do, in groups. One of them prays, the rest listen, and then they all partake. Did any of them actually commune with the Lord—or was that just a ritual? You have to get quiet before the Lord and wait on him.

Several years ago, I was given a very powerful prophetic dream regarding Communion, and I learned how he actually wanted it to be. I have provided that dream below. Go before the Lord with awe, respect, and reverence. Bring your completed repentance. Bring your personal repentance and the repentance for your ancestors. Offer praise and thanksgiving first and then wait upon the Lord. Ask him if there is anything he wants to tell you or show you. Ask if there is anyplace he would like to take you or any knowledge that he would like to press into you.

Tell the Lord that you are faithful, available, and teachable. Wait on him, and you will hear from him. In my experience, he does not answer immediately. That is why I recommend waiting upon the Lord. He will begin to communicate with you. Just listen. Read verse 24-25 out loud, present your completed petitions, and when you feel ready, partake of the elements. Ask the Lord to seal it in the blood of his precious Son, Jesus Christ.

Prophetic Dream: June 12, 2012

I was working with a younger man in the kitchen of a large church. We wore black rubber aprons and white T-shirts that were soaking wet with sweat and dishwater. It was very hot in there. The kitchen was actually part of the church building, and it had wide double doors that swung directly into the sanctuary.

The younger guy's dad, dressed in a white shirt and tie, opened up the double doors and shouted, "Come on. Get in here, both of you. Hurry. You have to see this!"

We both explained that we couldn't go in there dressed like we were.

He replied, "This is more important than how you are dressed. Hurry up and get in here."

We quickly did, but upon entering the sanctuary, we could not find him anywhere. The only thing that was going on was Communion. Up at the front, there were two lines of people. I got in one line, and he got in the other line. As we approached the altar, a lot of horseplay and pushing and shoving was going on behind us. People started cutting in line in front of us and bumping into us. They began to verbally mock the Communion service with total disrespect.

When it was my turn to partake, I saw that the cup of wine was actually a large drink of cranberry juice with crushed ice in it. The wafer was a large pastry with a chocolate tongue sticking out about half an inch from one side. I thought, *I will take this as a snack—but not as Communion. I'll take Communion for real when I get home.* I took the drink and the pastry and walked over to the opposite side of the sanctuary to consume it.

In the seats up above where I was standing, several people were mockingly singing, "It's time to get all the Jews. Let's round all of them up. The Jews' time is now up."

I didn't want to hear that, and I walked over to the coffee shop on the opposite side of the sanctuary. The kitchen, the sanctuary, and the coffee shop were all under one roof. When I walked in, a woman in a booth behind me said, "That's him. There he is!" She was dressed in a white gown with a headdress and a band around her forehead. Her headdress went up into a muted point, and a trail went down just below her shoulders.

She said hello to me, and I thought she might have been in a play or something based on the way she was dressed. I bid her hello and noticed that she had an insignia embossed on her gown. It closely resembled the New York Yankees insignia, and I wondered why she would be wearing a gown with a baseball team's insignia on it.

I walked up to her to get a better look at the insignia, which was embossed every four or five inches in a random pattern over the entire garment, and I noticed that the gown was extremely thin and made of a densely woven fabric. It reminded me of a lab coat that was thin enough to be worn straight out of the washer without even drying it. They would not hold a wrinkle or a blemish or spot because you could just wipe it off. The fabric was so dense.

Upon closer examination of the insignia, I saw a symbol that I had never seen before. I memorized the insignia, and then I woke up. I went straight into my office and scribbled the insignia on a yellow legal tablet. I went back to sleep, and when I woke up, I began to search the internet for this insignia. For some reason, I thought it was an ancient symbol for light. I searched the Hebrew alphabet, but I found nothing that resembled it. In my spirit, a voice said, "It's a word or a name—search it out" I continued to search, but I found nothing. That all happened on June 12, 2012.

On June 20, a woman was taking a Hebrew class at our church. I cut the insignia from the page in my tablet and gave it to her to show the instructor. She was shocked when he immediately informed her that it was ancient Hebrew for "Yahweh God."

I have taken Communion just as a ritual, not rightly discerning the blood and the body. I had known for a long time that the Communion service was not right in the churches, but I had no idea why or how to fix it. There was a time when I was actually afraid to take Communion because I did not want to drink damnation unto myself. That certainly was a stern warning in Corinthians. I thank God that he has granted me this benevolence and shown me all this truth.

Communion is not a ritual. It is not something to be taken lightly. It is not something to quickly get done so that you can move on.

I visited a church that designated one Sunday per month for Communion. It took all of ninety seconds to corporately commune with God. Ritual over! Let's go on to the next thing on our schedule.

I have been in churches where the Communion elements are available every Sunday for those desiring to partake. I have been in groups of eight or ten people all taking Communion at the same time while one of them leads a prayer. That is not communing with God; that is communing with each other.

I have also seen a lack of the fear of the Lord during Communion and even irreverence during the "ceremony." I knew these people did not know any better because they were never taught correctly. They also were not corrected for their behavior.

Do not trifle with the blood of Christ. It is the most valuable thing in the universe. It is more precious than all the gold and diamonds and everything else combined. Taking Communion in a manner that is unworthily brings judgment down on oneself. Take it correctly with fear and admonition of the Lord and realize that it is the body and blood of Christ and how precious that is to him. Take it in reverence and silence. Take your time with it. What does the Lord want to tell you? Just listen, wait on him, and commune with him. What do you want to settle with him?

For I have received of the Lord that which I also delivered unto you, that the Lord Jesus the same night in which he was betrayed took bread: and when he had given thanks, he brake it. And said, Take, eat: this is my body which is broken for you: this do in remembrance of me. After the same manner also he took the cup, when he had supped, saying, this cup is the new testament in my blood: this do ye as oft as ye drink it in remembrance of me. For as often as ye eat this bread and drink this cup ye do shew for Lord's death till he come. Wherefore whosoever shall eat this bread and drink this cup of the Lord unworthily shall be guilty of the body and blood of the Lord. But let a man examine himself and so let him eat of that bread and drink of that cup. For he that eateth and drinketh unworthily, eateth and drinketh damnation to himself not discerning the Lord's body. For this cause many are weak and sickly among you and many sleep. (1 Corinthians 23–30)

Please, dear saints, verse 27 tells us that we will be guilty of the body and the blood of the Lord. That is how precious Communion is to God. He will actually hold you guilty of the body and blood of his precious Son. This could cost you all.

SECTION III

Additional Sources of Curses

Curses That Proceed from the Mouth of God

God has the power to bless and curse—and so do you, which you have seen in previous chapters.

> See, I am setting before you today a blessing and a curse. The blessing if you obey the commands of the Lord your God that I am giving you today; the curse if you disobey the commands of the Lord your God and turn from the way that I command you today by following other gods, which you have not known. (Deuteronomy 11:26–28)

I have lived long enough to have seen these curses carried out in my own life as well as in hundreds of other people's lives. There can be no doubt about it. These curses will bring sickness, disease, financial damnation, failure, shame, mental breakdowns, relational difficulties, the breakdown of marriages, familiar alienation, and a host of other problems into your life and the lives of your descendants:

> And the Lord passed in front of Moses, proclaiming; The Lord, the Lord, the compassionate and gracious God, slow to anger, abounding in love and faithfulness, maintaining love to thousands, and forgiving wickedness, rebellion and sin. Yet he does not leave the guilty unpunished; he punishes the children and their children for the sin of the fathers to the third and fourth generation. (Exodus 34:6–7)

He is quick to forgive you, but he will in no way leave the guilty unpunished. I wish I knew that when I was a very young man, but I did not. If you only knew how heavy a price you will have to pay for your sins, you would not take sin so lightly. God does not take it lightly at all—and you will notice that even though he forgives you when you repent, you will still be punished. However, Sin that is repented for will not bring eternal judgment.

Curses That You Have Unknowingly Placed upon Yourself

These are mostly word curses that you have spoken that are in opposition to the will of God for you and that are actually harming you. You, above anyone else on earth, have the power to both bless and curse yourself.

Every time you utter negative things about yourself—to yourself or to others—you are cursing yourself. You are empowering this negativity to become a reality in your own life. You cannot blame Satan for that because that is actually your testimony of yourself. This has to be stopped immediately. There is power in your words, and this includes your positive and negative words. You are made in the image of God, and he framed the entire universe with his words. One of the most powerful gifts you have is the ability to use words—so begin to be more aware of what you say from this day on.

If you say, "I'm always broke, and I can't seem to save a dime," the "eavesdropping demons" will hear that and go to work to make that statement from your own mouth a lifelong reality. Unless you repent for that statement and all others that are not right in the eyes of God, you will actually live that out. I have lived through it, and I have seen many hundreds of others who have eaten the fruit of their very own tongues.

Every time we went to visit my uncle, he was always complaining about being a "pauper." I asked my dad what a pauper is, and I found out that it is someone who is broke. He complained about not having enough money all the time. He was actually obsessed about his "poverty lifestyle" and how he just could not get ahead, and he voiced it over and over again. I was just a kid, but I sure noticed his constant whining and moaning about a lack of money.

As I grew older, I noticed that the house they lived in was an extremely valuable property. I also knew they had a farm in another state that was quite a prize. He was groaning over his lack when he actually was worth well over two million dollars, and he didn't even know it! In fact, after his death, they sold "that old worthless farm" for a million dollars, but he did not see any of that money because he died in his fifties, broke, or so he thought and spoke. As a man thinketh in his heart, so is he.

Cease from all denigrating and disparaging words and phrases about yourself; otherwise, they will undoubtedly be carried out, very painfully, over your entire lifetime. You certainly do not need that—and neither do your children and grandchildren.

On the opposite side, start to use words that will bless you. You need to start looking at yourself the way that God sees you. He sees you through Jesus as complete and lacking nothing.

Curses Coming from the Servants of Satan

As Christians, we do not always know who is of God and who is of Satan. It takes special discernment to be able to distinguish between the people who are in God's kingdom and those who are in Satan's kingdom. There are those who have the gift of discernment of spirits. I have been blessed to know some of them. Just because we are all human does not mean that we are all alike. Don't be so naive that you think every person you meet is good—even in church. Be very careful about who you let lay hands on you and who you lay hands on.

I remember I was ministering at a prayer garden with a team of three other people. If anyone wanted a prayer, we would lay hands on them and pray for their needs. One night, a lady came up for prayer. I felt something was wrong, but I did not say anything to the others, mainly because the lady was standing right there. We all laid hands on her and began praying for her "marriage." The next day, I was sick. I was talking on the phone to another minister, and he told me that he was sick too. We thought it might have been something we ate, but we all ate dinner at home by ourselves before going out to minister.

I told him I would call the other two ministers to see if they were sick. When I found out both of them were sick too, I immediately knew the lady we had laid hands on was a witch. She was cursing us while we were praying for her. Her point of contact was our hands on her shoulders. A servant of Satan had been sent to the prayer garden to cause as much havoc as she could.

From that day on, I began to recite out loud the "breaking free" prayer to release me from anything negative that I might have picked up while interceding for others. That was not the first time something like that, or worse, had happened to me, but it was the last. This prayer has been my shield for many years now. I have given it to you here. It is also in the prayer section of this book.

Breaking Free Prayer

Lord Jesus, I thank you for the ministry of healing, deliverance, and intercession. I realize the evil, sickness, and disease that I have encountered today is more than my humanity can bear. I ask you to cleanse me of anything negative that I may have picked up while praying and interceding for myself and others. If any evil spirits have attempted to attach themselves to me or oppress me in any way, I break their power now. I cast them into the pit, and I seal them in there with the blood of Christ. As a king of the king and a priest of the priest, I decree that there will be no backlash, retribution, revenge, or spiritual retaliation leveled at me because of my prayers. I thank you, Jesus. Amen.

Curses Coming from the Servants of Satan

Witchcraft

This is much more common than many people think. I have been a victim of witches many times over the years, and I was not even aware of it. I never believed in witchcraft, and I thought those who did were just silly. I found out the hard way that I was wrong. Sometimes I remember feeling overwhelmed with problems and evil. I used to hunker down and wait until all the negative junk would pass. Most of the time, it lasted for several days. I just muddled through my day as best as I could, but I never equated the problems and feelings with witchcraft because I did not believe in it.

One of my first encounters with witches was in my youth. It was New Year's Eve, which is a very powerful holiday for witches. A neighbor dropped off two plates of tamales for us, and she said, "This plate is only for the man of the house." She handed it to me, and I gladly accepted. I began to eat the tamales, and I just loved them. I had never had tamales like that before. I started to feel embarrassed because I almost consumed an entire plate of them. I thought, *what is in these? They are so good.* I actually believed it was the best food I had ever eaten! I opened one up and saw what was in them. There were a bunch of animal eyeballs and other weird stuff. I opened up the other ones that were still left on my plate, and they were all the same. I opened the burritos on the plate she gave to the other people, and they were OK!

I told some people about it, and they said it was witchcraft. I believed it was the best food I had ever eaten because it was a cast spell. I threw the rest away, went over to her house, and yelled at her. I told her never to set foot in my place again.

Did I believe it was witchcraft? Yes, I knew it was—beyond a doubt. Did I believe it could harm me or have any effect on me? No, I did not because I did not believe in it. I thought it could have no effect on me at all.

A second encounter happened a few years later. I had a little shop behind my house, and I had six men working for me and producing machined parts. I had seventeen pieces of equipment in there. Everything had been going very well for several years until that particular day.

One of the guys came up to me and told me that his cutter had shattered. He could no longer run that job. When I took the cutter from him and examined it, I could not believe it could shatter like that. This cutter had cost more than six hundred dollars, and replacing it would take several weeks. It was a custom job, and I had no spare cutters. I told him to go over to another machine and start on those parts.

As soon as I redirected him, one of the other workers told me the machine he was using wouldn't turn on anymore. I checked, and it was completely dead. I checked the power and fuses, and I was dumbfounded. I sent him to another job on a different machine.

About fifteen minutes later, another guy told me that something had broken on his machine. He was stuck. I looked, and it was a broken part that I would have to replace. I was starting to get a little nervous. *Three jobs stopped within the hour. How could that be?*

The first guy came back and said his machine would not start anymore. He said, "What do you want me to do now?"

I was running out of options, but I sent him over to the saw to cut up some pieces of metal. Four pieces of equipment were down.

About forty-five minutes later, he told me the saw blade had broken.

I said, "Well, there are six more hanging on the wall right next to the saw."

He told me that he had broken all seven of the blades!

I was just standing there with all six of them, and they were asking what they should do. I said, "I know what you all should do. Just go home! There is plenty to do here, but we cannot do any of it at all."

They all left.

I was so upset. *This cannot be a coincidence. What is going on?*

I took a walk around the back of the building to cool off, and a neighbor was out there.

She came up to me and said, "Can I ask you a question?"

I said, "Sure."

She asked what all the little cardboard tubes that were surrounding my house and shop were for.

I said, "What tubes?"

She pointed them out to me.

I had been blinded to their presence. Every three feet, there was a small cardboard tube about the size of a person's thumb sitting upright, going around the entire property. I bent over to pick one up.

She said, "Don't bother. They are filled with dung. I already opened several of them up."

I thought, *OK, then, this is witchcraft—but how can it hurt me when I don't even believe in it?*

I called my mother, and she said, "It can't hurt you unless you believe in it."

Bad advice! I told her I didn't believe in it, but it had hurt me very badly.

I called somebody I trusted, and she told me that the cardboard tubes were a curse:

"May everything you do turn to dung." She asked if I had a horseshoe on a wall that was turned up in the shape of a cup.

I actually did have one on the outside wall of the shop.

She told me to get rid of it right away because they were directing curses into the horseshoe. I got rid of the horseshoe and the cardboard tubes, and I eventually got everything back in order. Still, I was rattled in my belief that I was immune to witchcraft because I knew now that I was not! I still did not know how to fight it off though—and that did not come until years later.

Curses from Those Who Are/Were in Authority over You

You do not have to receive words spoken to you from a person or persons who are in or were in authority over you. When I hear words spoken to me that are clearly in violation of me, I simply say to myself, "I do not receive that in Jesus's name."

Those in authority over us have power to invoke word curses upon us. In most cases, this is due to their ignorance. Your own parents may not have known that every word they spoke to you that was not right in the eyes of God had the potential to become a lifelong curse to you because they had the power to bless and to curse their very own children. I grew up under many word curses spoken by my parents—not out of malice but out of ignorance—and so did almost everyone else I knew. Their own parents did the same thing to them. This problem has been passed down through the generations, but you have the power to put a stop to it right now.

I had to go back in prayer to the Lord, root out all those word curses, and repent for my parents for saying them to me. I also to repent for any word curses that I unknowingly said to my own children and grandchildren. I wrote out my blessings to them and gave them to my children and grandchildren. I want to make you aware of the dangers of using improper words with your children and grandchildren. You will shape their lives in one way or another.

Other word curses can come from teachers, bosses, supervisors, doctors, or other authority figures. When I hear anything like that, my ears perk up because I am keenly aware of the dangers of word curses—and you will be too.

Ungodly Soul Ties

Ungodly soul ties need to be broken. They can affect your health and diminish your entire life as well as the lives of your descendants. These ties are created when engaging in sin with another person.

There are godly soul ties that are a blessing to you; in Genesis, Jonathan's soul was knitted to David's soul. This is a biblical example of a godly soul tie.

Ungodly soul ties include anyone you have had sex with outside of marriage because those acts created ungodly soul ties and need to be broken off. It also includes anyone who you have sinned with in any other way, such as drinking buddies, drug buddies, or participants in illegal activities or crimes. Use the list to go over everything and ask the Lord to show you where you have existing ungodly soul ties. He will do it for you just like he did in the breaking off of generational curses.

The procedure to breaking these off is the exact same procedure you used to break off generational curses. You have to acknowledge each and every one of these, repent for them, and break them off.

The Prayer

Lord God, I come to you today to acknowledge that I have sinned and unwittingly created a number of ungodly soul ties. I desire to break off each and every one of them. I break off the ungodly soul tie that I created with_____. I repent for this/ those sins (repeat each and every one of them), and I ask to be forgiven for it/them as I forgive myself. I ask that you wash this sin/those sins away in the blood of your precious Son, Jesus Christ, never to be remembered against me again. I know, Lord, that I will not be held accountable for these sins at my final judgment because those sins do not exist anymore. I ask to be released from the effects and consequences of my sin, and I ask that they do not perpetuate.

I give this person back everything I have that belongs to them, and I take back everything of mine that they have. In Jesus's name, I sever the cord that has bound us together, and I break off this ungodly soul tie in the blood of Jesus Christ. Amen.

SECTION IV

The Prayer Instructions

This section is a compilation of the prayers you will need in the pursuit you have undertaken. A brief explanation of these prayers is offered here. Remember to keep it clean. You need to keep your thoughts and speech clean, but did you know that you must keep your body and your home clean? If you were asking friends over, you would make sure you were clean, and your home was clean. How much more so if you are asking the Holy Spirit to come into your home!

The faithful, Available and teachable prayer, binding eavesdropping spirits prayer, and the setting the atmosphere prayer are a pathway into his throne room.

The praise, worship and thanksgiving prayer will open his gates. These four disciplines are a must before you enter into your prayer session.

Additional Prayers

Faithful, Available and Teachable

Here I am Lord, I am faithful, available, and teachable. If there is anything you want to tell me. If there is anything you want to show me, if there is anything that you just want to press into me, or anyplace you want to take me, I am here Lord waiting upon you.

If there is any other form of communication, in the supernatural that I am not aware of, I am willing Lord.

If there is anything outside the realm of communication that you desire, I am willing Lord.

Binding Eavesdropping Spirits

Lord Jesus, I thank you for taking me off the enemy's radar and off his frequency. I ask you to scramble my words today to you in prayer as well as my words to myself and anyone else—both oral and written—so that the enemy cannot eavesdrop on me and understand any of my communications. I now bind the enemy's eavesdropping spirits. I bind you spirits now and cast you into the pit. I seal you in there with the blood of Christ. I now loose the opposite spirits from heaven into my life instead. Thank you, Jesus. Amen.

Setting the Atmosphere

Lord God, if there be any spirits in this place that are evil, wicked, or demonic, I cast you spirits out now in the name of Jesus Christ. I cast you into the pit, and I seal you in with the blood of Jesus.

And, if there be any spirits in here that just do not belong here, I give you spirits leave and send you to the feet of Jesus for him to do with you as he will. I now loose the Holy Spirit into this place instead. I loose the sevenfold Spirit of the Lord, the Holy Spirit and helping spirits from you, Lord, as you would assign. Thank you, Jesus. Amen.

Praise, Worship, and Thanksgiving

Enter into your own praise, worship, and thanksgiving, you enter into his gates through praise, worship and thanksgiving.

Psalms 100:4 Enter into his gates with thanksgiving, and into his courts with praise: be thankful unto him and bless his name.

Only after this do you go into your prayer session.

Impenetrable Hedge of Protection

Father God, I ask you to put an impenetrable hedge of protection around me today for I have need of it. I ask you for an impenetrable hedge of protection to protect me from the attacks of the enemy, the demonic, the disembodied lost souls, the spiritual wickedness in high places, and the wicked people. I decree that a supernatural coat of resiliency cover me today so that any accusations or negative talk will have to slip right off. Father, I pray that if anyone says anything negative against me in any way or falsely accuses me of any supposed misdeed that no weapon formed against me or us will prosper (Isaiah 54:17). I bind the accuser, and I loose the opposite spirit into my life today. In the name of Jesus, amen.

Confess the Sins of Your Tongue

Lord God, I confess the sins of my tongue over the past day—or several days. I confess any and all words that I spoke that were words of idleness, words of foolishness, words that were agreeing with the enemy, and words that were faithless, blasphemous, profane, or untrue.

I confess any words that were unbecoming of me or even disparaging to me and any and all other words that were displeasing unto you. I confess them now as sin, and I renounce those words. I renounce each and every word that I spoke that was not right in your eyes. I recall those words from floating through the universe, and I send a detail of holy angels out to gather them up in nets and bring them back and bury them at the feet of Jesus.

I ask to be forgiven for those words, and I forgive myself and ask that those unfortunate words be washed away in the blood of your precious Son, Jesus Christ, never to be remembered against me again. So that I will not have to give an account for those words at the final judgment because they simply do not even exist anymore—even now.

Breaking Curses

This prayer is used primarily to defeat the servants of Satan and witchcraft. This is very important in the times in which we live. I have memorized it, and I use it almost every day. Since I was given this prayer—and I received it from the Lord one morning during my usual prayer session—I have experienced total victory over the enemy.

> Greater is he that is in you than he that is in the world. (1 John 4:4)

> Behold I have given you authority over all the power of the enemy. (Luke 10:19)

My experience using this prayer is proof of the truth of these two scriptures. I proclaim these two scriptures several times each week to the Lord, and I thank him for providing them to us.

Prayer

Heavenly Father, I silence and bind any and all curses that have been or will be cast at me today or over the past few days by the authority that I have to use the name of Jesus Christ and to apply his blood. Father, by the blood of Jesus, I renounce and break off any and all curses, spells, hexes, vexes, bewitchment, jinxes, hoodoo, voodoo, incantations, enchantments, satanic singing, and satanic chanting.

I break off the curses of disappointment, frustration and futility. Damage hurt pain and suffering. Sorrow, misery, and death. Confusion, confoundedness, consternation, mind fog, mind blinding, mind control, mind hindering and blocking, scattering, wandering, and any and all other mind control curses—even those that I may not be aware of at this time.

I break off the curses of not being able to see what I need to see, find what I need to find, get what I need to get, and comprehend what I need to comprehend.

I break off the curses of fear, rejection, torment, affliction, and damnation. Sadness, despair, negative thinking, hopelessness, anxiety, depression, repression, oppression by the enemy, any and all forms of bondage, and mental illness.

I break off the curses of automatic failure. I break off the curses of relational difficulties and familiar alienation.

I break off the curses of being my own worst enemy, everything I touch turns to dung. I break off the curses of all my efforts are in vain and all my good intentions going sour.

I break off the curses of financial damnation, poverty, and lack.

I break off the curses of sickness, disease, and poor health.

I break off the curses of bitterness, resentment, isolation, loneliness, humiliation, and defeat.

I break off the curses of losing gained ground, contests, competition, and court cases. I break off the curses of losing family and friends.

I break off the curses of losing money, valuables, property, assets, jobs, joy, happiness, and good health.

I break off the curses of losing respect, influence, time, opportunities, and any other commodities that I certainly would not want to lose—even though I may not be aware of them at this time.

I renounce and break off all these curses and any others that I am not aware of, including any unspoken, unknown, or hidden curses. Father, I reverse these curses back upon the heads of those servants of Satan who have cast them at me sevenfold (Psalm 109:17) in order to attack the kingdom of darkness and his servants and to rend them, stop them, scatter them, humiliate them, and defeat them. May they realize that by cursing me, they are only cursing themselves. I reverse all their evil words, actions, and deeds back upon their own heads, times seven, but If any of these people are appointed unto salvation, I cover them with the blood of Christ and with love and forgiveness, and I thank you, Lord, for saving them.

Lord, I replace these curses with your blessings. I call them forth in direct opposition to the curses I have just broken. May I be blessed in proportion to the cursing I have endured. I also call forth any unspoken, unknown, and hidden blessings. In Jesus's name, amen.

Protective Angels

Father, I call forth a detail of my holy protective angels to protect me and all my descendants and loved ones today wherever we go. Protect us when are at home, at work, or out and about. Protect us when we are driving in our cars with a supernatural angelic protective envelope surrounding our cars and angels on top of the car, in front and in back, and on each side of the car so that we cannot get into an accident or cause one.

Lord, I ask that you protect our food and water no matter where we get it from. Protect our tap water and electricity for we have need of it. Protect our bedding, shoes, clothes, books, furniture, appliances, and electronics. Protect our valuables and our intellectual property even from ourselves. I call for a detail of holy warring angels to stand shoulder to shoulder around all of us and around our families, homes, automobiles, jobs, schools, finances, health, and everything else that concerns each and every one of us, including the children.

I cover myself and my entire line of descendants and loved ones with the impenetrable, shed, and resurrected blood of Jesus Christ from the crowns of our heads to the soles of our feet, so that no harm may penetrate. In Jesus's name, I pray. Amen.

Breaking Free Prayer

Lord Jesus, I thank you for the ministry of healing, deliverance, and intercession, I realize the evil, sickness, and disease that I have encountered today is more than my humanity can bear. I ask you to cleanse me of anything negative that I may have picked up while praying and interceding for myself and others. If any evil spirits have attempted to attach themselves to me or oppress me in any way, I break their power now. I cast them into the pit, and I seal them in there with the blood of Christ. As a king of the king and a priest of the priest, I decree that there will be no backlash, retribution, revenge, or spiritual retaliation leveled at me because of my prayers. I thank you, Jesus. Amen.

Final Thoughts

Now that you have completed this book, cleansed and cleared your blood of all personal and ancestral sin, and forgiven everyone who has hurt you, you are in a unique position of freedom and righteousness. I urge you to protect that status by reviewing your life from time to time as the Lord leads and doing updated personal repentance. I usually do this at least three times per week in order to keep clean. You will probably be reminded by the Lord of other ancestral sins as you go through life, and I advise you to deal with them right away. As far as forgiving others, that has to be done on a regular basis. Please do not let any of this build up—and handle them in prayer right away.

Remember to pray the Sins of the Tongue prayer to tame your tongue. This is very important because you do not want to be held accountable for every idle word that you have ever spoken (Matthew 12:36). In your prayer time, bring up your word transgressions to the Lord and renounce, repent, and recall them to keep your speech clean.

You have something very valuable to you and your family here, and I don't want you to lose it or take it lightly. Section III ("Sources of Curses") educates you and makes you aware of these possible threats.

I want you to read and study Deuteronomy 27 and 28; this is where the Lord lays out blessings and cursing for you to choose.

Stay within the boundaries set by the Ten Commandments. Study Proverbs and Psalms since they have enlightenment and wisdom to keep you upright.

Finally, remember that in order to qualify to be a son or daughter of God, you have to hear his voice and follow his commandments. It is not enough to just believe that God sent Jesus as his only begotten Son, claim to be a Christian, or go to church each week. That is all good to be sure, but to actually be a son or daughter of God, that falls to "as many as hear my voice and follow my commandments." These are the words of Jesus himself.

Some of my harshest lessons in life came as a result of assuming I was a partaker of the promises of God and his blessings, and when things did not go my way, I became angry at God. I thought, *is this the way you treat your children? Where are you?* I believed in God and Jesus, and I went to church, but it could not be said that I was a child of God because I did not hear his voice or keep his commandments. Well, I kept most of them, but I found out that is not enough.

What is the result of this failure? It can lead to rebellion, and rebellion is as the sin of witchcraft. I began to think that God is so far away that he doesn't seem to know or care about what happens to his people. I would pray and give part of my finances, but I received nothing except silence. My rebellion began to grow and grow. A person in that condition is the perfect target for the demonic and those ministries that feed upon "hurting people." You cannot "give" your way to prosperity and wellness. I have seen hundreds of people who attempted to do so, including myself, but it does not work. Giving is admirable to be sure, but it will not—on its own—change your life. Qualifying to be a son or daughter of God will.

If God is not there for you, it's because you are not seeking him with all your heart. You need to develop a close personal relationship with him, talk to him every day, and get sin and rebellion out of your life. The Lord will use calamity and the bad things that happen to good people to get your attention. Did you ever consider that? It's true. Never run from God; instead, run to him.

Repenting for your own personal sins and the sins of your ancestors, getting sin out of your life, and thoroughly forgiving others will reverse things for you.

My testimony to you is that once I did all this, I began to see that every promise in the Bible came true for me. I recognized that all the wisdom, revelation, and knowledge was available to me because I qualified for it—and now so do you!

For questions or comments, to order more workbooks for in-home Bible studies, gifts for family and friends, or discipleship classes at your church or in your bookstores, contact the author, Wendell Wayne Gilkey Jr., at holybloodtransfusion@gmail.com.

Printed in the United States
by Baker & Taylor Publisher Services